Compelling Evidence for God

Thinking Your Way to Truth

Ray W. Lincoln

Apex Publications
Ingram, TX

Compelling Evidence for God
Thinking Your Way to Truth

© 2020 by Ray W. Lincoln
All rights reserved.

No part of this book may be reproduced or transmitted in any form or by any means, electronic or mechanical, including photocopying, recording, or by any information storage and retrieval system, except as may be expressly permitted by the 1976 Copyright Act or in writing from the publisher. Requests for permission can be addressed to Permissions, Apex Publications, 520 Chestnut Oak, Ingram, TX 78025-3284 or emailed to solutions@raywlincoln.com.

Library of Congress Cataloging-in-Publication Data has been requested.

ISBN: 978-0-9996349-4-3

Manufactured in the United States of America

Acknowledgements

Originality is hard to find. This book is not original in any absolute sense but has been shaped by the writings of significant authors, some of whom lived a long time ago and have left for us their arguments and insights. To all those authors who have given me the benefit of their thoughts and who have molded my thinking — both those I have agreed with and those who have stimulated my thinking with their contrary beliefs — I owe my gratitude. There are too many through the years to even remember and thank, of course.

Many people, some long forgotten, have also influenced me with their convictions. But their impact on my thinking remains, causing important changes for which I am profoundly thankful. I wish I could show my appreciation in a more meaningful way to all of these, too.

So thank you all. But a sincere thanks to those who have labored with me more closely in this task. My dear wife must have special mention because she has worked so efficaciously and has been responsible for all the details that must be accomplished to bring this book to life.

To you, the reader, it is my hope that your beliefs will be bolstered and firmly established in the face of the overwhelming evidence I seek to provide. As a result, may your life be given a yet more vibrant expression of the image in whom you have been made.

Ray W. Lincoln.

Contents

The First Big Question 5
The Evidence for God 15
Evidence From Design 15
The Human Body — Designed? 15
The Design Argument 17
More Design Found in Just One Human Organ 18
DNA and Epigenetics 20

1973 — A Revolutionary Discovery 25
"The Anthropic Principle" 25
Shock Waves 26
Takeaways 26

Science Responds 31
A Theory of Everything 32
Many Universes 34

In Conclusion 39
Let's Focus On Intelligence 39
Let's Focus on the Implausible Nature of Random Happenings ... 40
Let's Focus on What Chance Cannot Do 41
Let's Focus on Whether We Can Happily Live Knowing We Are Creatures of Chance? 41

Introduction

Is there a God? Was the universe intelligently designed? Or has the universe developed by unintelligent, natural, random happenings that created life itself and a vast universe by evolving over billions of years? Is there any overwhelming evidence one way or the other? Does it matter?

These are some of the big questions that underlie our understanding of the world and everything in it. They influence how we live and how our lives will be molded; and yes, they do matter — a lot. Our beliefs actually shape our lives. This book (the first in a series of books dealing with the questions that have exercised the best minds throughout the ages and plagued all sincere seekers after truth) deals with questions that must be answered. Its message is for anyone, but its inspiration came from the many questioning teens and from their parents, who wanted more understanding of the big questions of life to share with their teens before they entered college.

Here's a typical teenage perspective…

> *I'm a teen and I will be going off to college soon. I'm told it's great, but I don't know what to expect. My parents don't seem to know, either, but they keep encouraging me to get educated. They grew up in a world really different from mine. They didn't even have smartphones when they went to college. Weird! Can you believe it? My grandparents must have lived in an uncivilized era because they hadn't even seen a cell phone when they were kids. How did they communicate?*
>
> *I'm slowly becoming aware that the world is changing fast, driven by ever-changing philosophies and beliefs — ideas about what is true and what isn't. I'm full of*

questions, like "why do people say there's no such thing as absolute truth?" Is there something wrong with me? Am I missing something? Isn't that statement an absolute statement? Am I not also being told <u>it</u> is true? I think that means it is an absolute truth, and there's not supposed to be any such thing? Obvious contradiction? I guess so. But perhaps I'm not as smart as those who believe it. I'd like to know if it's really truth, though.

Have I ever stopped to think, "Is there a God?" Well, it has crossed my mind, briefly. But does it really matter — if you don't want to be religious, I mean? Does it even matter <u>what</u> we believe at all, or only how we feel and what we do? People keep saying to me, "Just follow your heart." That's another puzzle. My feelings keep changing. To me, that offers no real north star to guide me.

When I look at the stars, I wonder where the universe came from. They say it just happened after a giant explosion. That's what I hear most. Oh yes, and which is true: the Bible and God creating it all, or the Big Bang and whatever happened after that? I'd like some solid answers, if there are any. I also still really wonder at times who I am in the grand scheme of things. That's another big question. How should we live? Or is that a stupid question?" I mean, do we make up our guidelines as we go along or where do we find some really good ones? I'd like to know, too: can we really answer those big questions? Or do we simply go through life shaped by the gadgets we can buy and play with, or the needs of the moment, wondering who we are and if living is really worth the trouble? I feel kind of mixed up and afraid at times."

This is a call to know <u>why</u> we believe <u>what</u> we believe.

Parents and the rest of us have a great opportunity to help not just teens, but all who wonder. They don't need glib answers. Rather, solid evidence with intelligent reasoning about the big questions. At times, parents feel inadequate to defend their own beliefs or talk intelligently to their teens. Is it important what they believe as long as they are good kids? Absolutely!

Children think and feel differently from their parents because they continually absorb, by osmosis, the culture and beliefs around them — a culture very different from the culture of their parents' early days. Parents often don't realize how different their children are in the way they think. The answers our youth are going to accept are either what they get outside the home or what will be taught with solid evidence and logic from within the home. Their beliefs will shape their lives and mold the influence they will, in turn, have on society at large. So this book is for you, parent, young person or anyone who shares the concerns raised by the plethora of beliefs out there today.

When our children go to college and the professor scoffs at a belief we parents taught them, who do we think they believe? Who is the obvious expert? Students loose their beliefs fast in college and university and come out with beliefs that quite honestly are nothing but the latest baked philosophy, hot out of the oven of yet another half-baked culture. Often, these postmodern beliefs are soon to be found lacking, leaving the puzzled graduates feeling empty and confused. A strange undercurrent of uncertainty and doubt then settles in when they face life's trials. Their beliefs (or lack of a solid belief) are, to their dismay, inadequate for life's challenges We need more than just a faith of the heart and an experience that warms us. We need a head knowledge that satisfies the demands of our intelligence. I will attempt in these pages to begin to meet these needs.

On our journey we will discover that Professor Dr. William Daley and his book *Natural Theology* have been scorned and repudiated for their belief in a God who was both creator and designer of this vast and intricate universe. However, as the years have rolled by and the scientific evidence has mounted, his army of critics have been stained with embarrassment and not a little shame over their unintelligent eagerness to get rid of a belief that amounted to nothing but unintelligent opinions.

We will also find out in this series that everyone has a "faith" of some sort that shapes their lives. It matters a lot what we believe, but our beliefs also need to be grounded in real solid evidence. And we are about to find out where that evidence is to be found.

So, we are about to tackle the question: Is there a God and did he create this vast and intricate universe? Yes, we will find out.

The footnotes are for those who want more explanation and information. Otherwise, just ignore them. The bibliography is for those who want to read a selection of sources for these arguments that I provide and for those who want to wrestle with these great metaphysical arguments. Check the vast notes and bibliographies in each book for complete research.

The First Big Question

Today, all secular philosophers and others, of course, laugh condescendingly at the opening words of the Bible, "In the beginning God created the heavens and the earth."[1] But who's having the last laugh? We'll find out!

Let's start with an examination of those words: "In the beginning God created the heavens and the earth." What are they trying to tell us?

There are two thoughts here.

1. The first is: "In the beginning **God.**" If you accept and believe there is a God, then you are called a theist (the word comes from the Greek word for God, *theos*). Reject the idea that there is a God and you are called an atheist. Theism is the belief in one God. Atheism is the belief in no God. The "a" before the word theist, **a**theist, simply means I do not accept that there is a God. All the world-views and beliefs that do not accept that there is a God are atheistic in nature.

2. The second thought contained in the opening words of the Bible is that God acted in the beginning and "**created the heavens and the earth.**" The words "created the heavens and the earth" point to where the evidence for the truth or falsehood of a belief in God can be found. So, God took a step toward revealing to us whether he existed or not. That step was to do something, create something that we could examine

---

[1] Genesis 1:1. I have chosen to examine these opening words of Genesis because they are once again at the center of the religious/secular debate over origins. They call for acceptance or rejection, forming an intersection for our beliefs that cannot be circumnavigated and at which all discussions about the beginning of the universe will sharply diverge.

to see if he was indeed God and worthy of our faith. Therefore, the heavens and the earth become the arena for our examination and is also the vast field in which science operates. Science observes and discovers the world, our universe, and everything in it that can be examined and tested to see what it tells us. This is science's self-appointed task, a noble and worthy task for which we can be thankful.

Proof or Evidence — Which?

Science is to many people their religion because it is what they seem to believe more than anything else. So let's ask, can we scientifically prove there is a God? Answer: NO!

Why?

Because we can't scientifically examine something that is not made of an examinable substance and the God of the Bible does not exist in an examinable form. He has no physical existence; he is spirit, unobservable and untouchable and, therefore, outside of the reach of scientific examination.

But don't forget, the atheist cannot scientifically prove there is NO God, either, for exactly the same reason! So when the atheist shouts at the theist, "You cannot prove that there is a God," he has just undermined his own stance if he declares that he can prove there is no God.

Which Faith?

So how do both theism (belief in God) and atheism (belief that there isn't a God) come to their respective conclusions if we can't prove the matter one way or the other? By an act of faith. In other words, what the individual <u>chooses</u> to believe for whatever reason! And on what basis do they choose? Both would answer "on the evidence that is observable in the heavens and the earth" — evidence that can be examined.

So, what evidence might we expect to find if there is a God and God did in fact create the universe?

Before you proceed, read the whole first chapter of Genesis, which is in the form of a poem. When you read it without a predetermined bias, you should be at least mildly impressed at the order in which the creation took place. It is an order that makes sense and has been shown to be a necessary order. The creation of this universe could not have happened if verses 19-25 happened before verses 2-18, for example. And I'll leave you to find more examples of the right order, if you wish. The beginnings of the evidence of intelligent design (and certainly not of random happenings guided only by chance with no forethought and planning[2]) are seen in the order these verses take.

---

[2] The words *intelligence, purpose* and *design* are used here as meaning the opposite of the words *random, chance, hit or miss,* or *luck.* Intelligence has the ability to understand what it is doing, to reason, and to know and comprehend, therefore to plan and thoughtfully create. It cannot be the property of inanimate matter (the dust of the ground, for example cannot think). It is the property of mind. Therefore, its opposite — randomness, as it is used here — does not have the ability to act as the result of some existing condition. It is haphazard. Purpose is acting with a goal, end or aim in mind. Designing is the mental act of planning or of acting out a purpose, to create, or to decide a specific function or outcome.

There is evidence of purpose here, too. God made all this for a purpose, which turns out at the end of the chapter to be the creation of humans. He made humans, both male and female, "in his [own] image" it says.[3] That statement is the climax of the chapter and we will note its significance later. The reason for man being the purpose or end of creation emerges in the second and third chapters. It is so that God could have a relationship with them. He is seen as wanting to communicate with both the man and the woman and establish a meaningful relationship of trust. God is also pictured as making everything for man's (humanity's) enjoyment.

So the account tells us, if this is a fair reading, that we (science) will find a creation that is intelligently and purposefully designed. It is also necessary to find overwhelming evidence of these things throughout all of creation if these opening words of the Bible are to be correct.

The opposite, a random development of the universe[4], would give evidence that life and all of creation evolved by natural selection or some method other than intelligent design, and it would not matter how long it took — over however many years. The various theories of the origin of the species — or the origin and development of the entire universe by some form of evolution that excludes intelligent, purposeful design — have been the bread and butter of the atheists' explanation of how the universe came to be.

---

[3] This claim we will examine, along with the evidence for it, later when we ask the question, "Who am I?"

[4] A "random universe" was the watchword of science in the past and is often still the belief of those who teach in our universities, educating our youth. However, it has long since lost its significance in the face of design being found and depended upon in our scientific laboratories and in the application of medical science, for example. The understanding and importance of design is evident in all the sciences and is crucial to philosophy that cannot reasonably bypass its significance.

Our Thesis In a Nutshell

It is my thesis that we have found and will find overwhelming and convincing evidence of purposeful design in the universe and, as a result, we will have verified the claim of the opening words of the Bible, closing the door to all theories of how the universe began and evolved that claim it did so randomly by chance happenings or simple adaptation from existing conditions [5]. If overwhelming evidence of purposeful design were not to be found, then we will have shown the opening statement of the Bible to be false, and the door is wide open to any and all speculations.

Atheism has only one avenue of proof for its claims, and that is to show convincing and overwhelming evidence of a random (as opposed to an intelligently designed) universe. When we remove an intelligent source, we are left with unintelligence. Surprisingly, when atheistic minds are clinging to their theories, scientists are finding evidence of design and mindful purpose everywhere. The scientist's laboratory is where lots and lots of it is showing up daily. It is an undeniable fact of nature.

Even Darwin did not deny that there was evidence of design in creation. However, he sought to deny its obvious message by proving that the design we see in nature is only giving us an appearance of design and that, in its place, blind and progressive adaptation (natural selection) over billions of years mimics the effects that intelligence would produce. Really?

So I have five main questions for Mr. Darwin...

1. Why did you use your intelligence to tell us ("us" including you, of course) we are the product of an unintelligent process? Does this not feel like you are using something that an unintelligent

---

[5] Scientists in three main areas are finding more and more evidence of design. Those areas of study are: cosmology, biochemistry and biological information derived from the study of DNA and its related sciences.

process logically could not create — namely, intelligence? Further, Mr. Darwin, where did your intelligence come from and how could your unintelligent process of evolution have produced intelligence? Simply put, if you are a creation of an unintelligent process, you cannot claim to possess intelligence?

2. Isn't intelligence the opposite of blindness and progressive adaptation?

3. Am I wrong in thinking that intelligence contains qualities that blindness and principles of adaptation simply don't have and that even an aeon of time cannot endow to them? Is this not a form of logical suicide to attribute intelligence to blind forces?

4. How is it that the design we see on a mind-boggling scale can be reduced to a blind process of natural adaptation? Could it have happened without any advances in the evolution of a human being and imperfectly timed? Imagine the result of eyes forming before the nerve connections to all the areas of the brain that are needed for the eye to be useful. What would happen to this improperly functioning person who has no working eyes? Natural selection alone, evolving over the billions of years you give it without an overall plan is, it seems to me, a certain disaster. And is it feasible to think all this amazing design was created without an ultimate goal and purpose in "mind"? Don't you know that a simple cell, nucleus and all, must be created as a complete functioning whole or it will die before it is finished; and all the time it is being made, it must be fed its nutrients to keep it alive? Then how could that be done over a long period of time without disaster striking? Sorry. I didn't realize blind, natural adaptation had such a brilliant mind and obvious intelligence.

5. Can I safely assume that intelligence is for the purpose of achieving what blind natural forces at work cannot achieve?

Darwin and his followers have been at pains to convince us that design as we see it on such a vast scale in both the macro and micro universe is not real. We are supposed to believe it is merely a deception. Natural section, they tell us, makes it look like an intelligent design when it is just the result of chance happenings.

They have a hard road ahead of them and have not yet even begun to convince those who see obvious cases of design as a true result of an intelligent mind. Darwin and those who still cling to his conclusions pursue a futile word game, trying to convince us while we are learning more and more about the astounding design in this universe.

We are told by biochemists that the cell is a stunning design of high-tech, molecular activity more amazing than anything we humans have engineered. Perhaps if Darwin had known what we know today, he would not have even thought of writing his book, *The Origin of the Species*.[6] More on evolution later.

A Few Facts About Religions

Now, it's obvious that there were no observers to verify the Bible's opening claims. If these claims are true, they must be regarded as revelations from the God who created the heavens and the earth. Who else would be a dependable witness? The pen that wrote these words would have been inspired by God.

At the beginning of our investigations we should also note two things.

First, the Judaeo/Christian religions are the only religions that claim there is a God who is a *person* (the source of all personhood) and who is also *intelligent* (the source of all intelligence). All the other religions and philosophies face the daunting task of explaining the evidence we are discussing and the origin of our world without shifting to a purposeful intelligent mind behind it all.

---

[6] For more detailed evidence see, Michael Behe, *Darwin's Black Box, The Biochemical Challenge to Evolution*.

Second, most people think all religions believe in a God or gods, plural. They do not. Buddhism, Taoism, and Confucianism are examples. Some other faiths (pantheism and New Age, for example) define deity as a mere force within the universe, somewhat like the "force" in Star Wars movies; or a God who has no interest in what happens to the universe he created; or one that does not have the qualities of mind, hardly fulfilling the common meaning of the word God.

So what separates the Christian and Jewish religions from all others is this fundamental belief in God as an intelligent person. The teachings of the Bible make no sense if there isn't a God who is an intelligent person and who also created the heavens and the earth.[7]

Why Doesn't God Want to Step Up to the Plate and Settle the Matter?

Why doesn't God, if he exists, show himself and get the matter settled once and for all?

Because God wants a relationship with us. Trust or faith is the foundation of any meaningful relationship. Remove the need for faith and trust and you have stripped a relationship of its heart. We

---

[7] All people have an answer to the question of what is their ultimate explanation for life and the universe, even if it is absorbed by a kind of osmosis from the surrounding culture or the presuppositions embedded and hidden in their intellectual training. Many have never thought it through and I have found some who have been highly educated among these. This ultimate explanation of all things is also the foundation for their moral choices. But often, they find their bearings in life by borrowing meaning from another ultimate explanation, such as when an atheist believes in love — which they unwittingly borrow from God (who is a person and the true and only really consistent answer to where true love came from) — and not a dry chemical neurosis that has emerged and produced all the elements of true love.

never enter into a relationship without the need for some faith; we never know everything about our prospective partner or about the future the relationship may face, either. So, a lack of trust nullifies the efficacy of the relationship.

Trust is the proof of our intent to enter meaningfully into a relationship. "Taste and see that the Lord is good," declares the Psalmist. "Believe," insists Jesus. Faith in God is the first requirement for finding the reality of God in our own experiences. God wants faith and trust from us so that the relationship becomes efficacious and has heart. The necessity of trust cannot be avoided, and again let me emphasize: God wants it that way. Remember, he is a person and we, also, being persons like he is a person, want it that way in our relationships.

We Will Settle These Two Questions

Whether we are going to side with the atheist and materialistic, scientific beliefs or the Bible's opening statement is further defined by asking the following two questions.

1. Which belief does the evidence found in the heavens and the earth point to overwhelmingly?

2. Which belief best fits life as we know it?

These questions can be intelligently discussed because they can be observed and their effects tested in a study of the universe and all that is in it? By doing so we can remove unwanted, unwarranted speculations, and there are many of those being proposed in our current culture and, surprisingly, used in intellectual arguments.

We will also consider, among other things, the following:

1. Is there any evidence that nullifies the arguments of either belief?

2. Which can be consistently and meaningfully lived on its own claims without self-contradiction?

The Evidence for God

Now we move to where the evidence is found: "In the beginning God **created the heavens and the earth**".

Evidence From Design

If it is true that the universe shows clear evidence of design, then there must have been an intelligent designer involved in its creation and development. A cause cannot produce a result greater than its own inherent nature. In other words, an intelligent design cannot be created by unintelligence or a state that exhibits no intelligence, like random chance happenings.

To believe that unintelligence can create intelligence or randomness can create design, particularly on an overwhelming scale, is to deny the principles of logic. That belief also amounts to a giant leap of faith into the unknown far greater than a belief in God and asks us to believe the unbelievable. It also begs all the principles essential to intelligent design. Design requires order, pre-thought and planning, a purposeful goal the designer moves toward — such as producing something that is useful, like a car or a stove. A functioning design requires even more, such as sustainability, reliability, and in the case of designing living creatures, reproductive capabilities as well.

The Human Body — Designed?

The human body is just one example we can use from what we find in the heavens and the earth. Billions or trillions of cells make up the human body and function with amazing reliability over a lifetime. They malfunction very little in comparison to what we know of their dependable functioning, and then mostly when mismanaged. Accidents, internal and external influences from substances damaging to their reliable operation, and simple misuse and abuse are the main causes of the comparatively few malfunctions.

Is there a purpose and design to the human body that the medical and psychological sciences seek to restore to its original design when it malfunctions or is damaged? Of course. Then why doesn't this amazing evidence of design found in our bodies comprise an overwhelming proof that this universe is not a concoction of random happenings but is purposefully created by a designer? The only objection seems to be from those who must prove to themselves, if not also to others, that there is no creator God.

Looking at the human body, we further notice it is an astounding assemblage of systems: cardio, neural, defense, maintenance, mental and psychological, immune, energy, development or growth, digestive, reproductive, plus heating and cooling systems, to name only a few. How could all these systems with their myriads of cells and chemicals, neurotransmitters, enzymes, healthy bacteria and other needed elements, all controlled via a mind/brain, have happened any other way than by design? Biochemistry alone produces convincing evidence.

Even given billions of years for its development, it begs belief that all these came together to form a living cell without purpose, plan or design, at precisely the right time, in the right order — not one appearing before another so as to create obstruction for other systems or elements to function — and each according to their own purposes.

The complexity of a single cell and the need for all of it to be in place to function as designed can now be seen to our amazement, thanks to high-tech electron microscopes. What we see of its functioning warrants the description of being an irreducible complexity[8]. Any concept that suggests a cell comes into being without a predetermined, complex plan or that it can be reduced in any way and still perform its task has been disproved. To believe all this happened randomly is far more incredible than to believe it is the result of intelligence. It is impossible. And besides, where did the thing called life that moved all of this to a planned goal, creating a living pulsing cell full of bustling "organized chemical activity"[9] come from? Are we not staring intelligence in the face?

The Design Argument

The argument from design is, not surprisingly, one of the oldest. That's because it is one of the strongest arguments and, for us, one that is expanding in strength almost daily.

---

[8] Michael Behe illuminates this point by citing the construction of a mousetrap. Here is a summary of some of his reasoning. Building the human system is like building a mousetrap. It cannot be built haphazardly. Parts must be assembled to create a whole. No mice are caught until all the parts are in place. First it must have a base, then a spring and hammer mechanism with a trigger system and the application of bate. Reduce its complexity by omitting one or more parts and the trap catches no mice. Assemblage requires the completion of the whole project without one piece missing — an irreducible complexity. It must be built according to a blueprint and a plan and assembled as a whole. To think that the highly complex functioning of a human cell had no blueprint and plan and was assembled piecemeal over billions of years is unthinkable. Blueprint, plan, designed assemblage and an irreducible complexity are all essentials for success or the cell cannot come into existence and fulfill its purpose. Even Darwin admitted that if biology showed a complexity that could not be reduced, his theory of evolution would be destroyed. The evidence of irreducible complexity has been demonstrated.

[9] Francis Crick, famous for his work with DNA, uses the phrase "organized chemical activity" to describe the astounding, complex functioning of a single cell. He also calls a cell a "minute factory" because of the many manufacturing functions it performs. It is a miniature manufacturing town.

In 1802, Dr William Paley, professor at Cambridge University in England, in his book *Natural Theology* penned the analogy of a watch[10]. He argued: "If you happened upon a watch, sitting on the ground, and you had never seen or heard of a watch before, would you think, after careful examination and analysis, that it happened by chance or that there was somewhere a thoughtful designer that had fashioned it with a purpose?" The common sense or main point of this analogy has never been refuted even though ingenious arguments have been formed to try and show it has nothing to do with the equally common sense argument that design in the universe indicates a designer. It's the believable common sense of this analogy that is my point. Do you get it?

Design is everywhere in our bodies and in the entire universe. We live only because we are designed to live. To suggest that life and this body are easily explained by natural forces randomly at work is, pardon me, insane. The full intricacy of it all is still beyond us and being progressively discovered by science daily. This should comprise for us a sufficient and conclusive argument that an intelligent designer was involved. We all know the body has a design because every day we feed and nurture it so that it will function according to its known design. Every day, it declares the existence of a designer, not the haphazard result of chance, accidents or unplanned natural selection.

More Design Found in Just One Human Organ

We'll choose one organ of the body to argue design: our brains, which most of us make use of daily (pardon my humor)!

---

[10] William Paley published his most influential work, *Natural Theology or Evidences of the Existence and Attributes of the Deity in 1802*. In it he reasoned the matter of design as consisting of irrefutable evidence for God's existence.

Our brains are made of fatty tissue — mostly cholesterol — and weigh about three pounds. It is estimated that there are about ten billion tiny neurons or nerve cells in the brain, connected by a vast mileage of communication channels — including axons, dendrites, a complete nerve system network — making connections to all parts of the body, and a vast system of blood vessels that feed the cells and perform maintenance duties. The synapses (gaps where neurotransmitters function) and other forms of connections in the brain are said to be in excess of the number of stars in the Milky Way. Impressed?

This brain is the key organ of the body — "Grand Central Station," if you like — and in one way or another it keeps in efficient touch with the estimated one trillion cells of the human body — constantly. Messaging systems to and from this central station receive and send signals, working around the clock and lasting for a lifetime. Damaged cells are replaced and new cells that are required for new neural pathways are created as stem cells and then migrate to needed areas where they are initialized for service. (Is there no intelligence and purposeful design in this?) Both incoming and outgoing messages are all evaluated and acted upon even when interrupted by our sudden changes of mind and our unexpected choices. All that must keep the system on its toes!

Of course, all this is happening to achieve multiple effects and purposes, and the brain is intricately and constantly handling our personally directed thoughts like no computer we have created can even dream of doing. Please help me understand why we firmly believe a computer was designed by intelligent, ingenious minds, but the brain, (which is far more complex) happened by unintelligent, random activity — a process instigated by inanimate forces that can't even think — as we unfortunately have been educated to believe?

Yes, and there is more. The brain diligently fights off its enemies, such as free radicals and inflammation, running an impressive in-built self-repairing system. Note this please: all of this without having to call in an outside technician.

Our habits and thinking change more in some of us than in others. Therefore, let's not forget, our brains can handle virtually anything we can throw at it, creating new mental circuits and growing these circuits as needed and directed, literally changing the landscape of the brain in a split second whenever we change our minds. It stores an amazing amount of data for our recall and can reason and make judgements like no computer can, always taking into account the complex operation of our endless emotional choices, their values and, incidentally, values that keep changing, which is perhaps its most complex mental process.

DNA and Epigenetics

To convince you yet more, let's go inside one of those minute brain cells. (I will simplify what we have found). There is a skin (membrane) we will need to penetrate and, after passing by numerous molecules all performing their own tasks, we reach the nucleus of the cell. Once inside the nucleus, we will find our DNA, a complete copy in every cell. But this is a very changeable world we experience. We are subject to changes that can help us and other changes that can hurt or even destroy us. Therefore, as Epigenetics is teaching us, about 70 percent (the number varies) or more of the genes can alter the way they are expressed. It has focused on certain parts of our DNA, called *marks,* that instruct our genes how strongly or when to express themselves.

We can personally influence the operation of these genes by our choices and our thoughts — a feature random selection cannot explain because choices are not random; they are purposeful. Our daily activities or lifestyle also profoundly influence how our genes express themselves, requiring them to change to accommodate our lifestyle needs and choices ad infinitum, if needed. Note, most of these changes are activated by our thoughts, conscious and unconscious, something I have been making my brain do over the last few hours. When you think about it, that we can do this is convincing evidence of purposeful, intelligent design. The material and the immaterial are both involved in the functioning of our mental system.

While we are also interacting with a world that is constantly messing with our stress loads, and while we make poor lifestyle choices, suffer unexpected shock, and try to deal with our day (which will never be totally the same as yesterday or tomorrow), our mental system manages to keep up with it all. And to think that our DNA, amazing in itself, is this busy trying to take care of it all, it presupposes great intelligence and a physical, creative result beyond our wildest imagination — all repeated trillions of times and embedded successfully in our systems.

Question: How can purposeful activity be created by a process that lacks understanding of what is going on and has no idea of what it is supposed to be doing?

More on Neurogenesis

Neurogenesis has shown that we create new brain cells to replace damaged ones or to increase our mental abilities and meet our needs and desires all throughout our lives.

We can create new communication circuits in our brains, and highly complicated ones at that. By the way, we can make existing ones stronger, too. Ever noticed that you strengthen what you want and not the thought patterns you don't want and don't use? All this is directed by an intelligent response to our thoughts, actions and wishes.

The evidence continues to mount up when we consider these new revelations from science. Let's not forget: (ironically for some scientists) science is strengthening our belief daily in the amazing design we find in this universe inside of our bodies. Our brains and the tissues of our bodies, from liver to hair, continue to create new cells and connections with other cells and rely on this designed process to meet our needs for growth (which if not designed and is only random, could destroy us any moment, any time). Be very happy that randomness is not how we came into being or how we function daily.

How does it happen by chance that we develop a clear understanding of our needs? If you believe in human evolution, undirected by intelligence, it looks like you will have to admit that the overwhelming evidence of design that you must exclude from consideration in your quest to find randomness is a rather hypocritical exercise.

Our understanding of neurogenesis blossomed in the 1990s. In 1998 we learned from the Swedish neuroscientist Eric Erikson of the constant regeneration of stem cells in the brain that can become new neurons, functioning for whatever purpose the brain requires, not randomly. Its frequency is my next point. This happens daily, in fact hourly, for all our lives — some say, by the minute. A computer is static and does not grow itself. Life (with its intelligent, purposeful actions) and random, inert happenings are poles apart in their definitions and functions.

Those who believe in a random universe must face the question of design or randomness (and it doesn't matter what form the suggested randomness takes; it is still random) and not continue kicking the question down the road into the future, saying, "We will have an answer someday," when all the evidence already points to the answer of intelligent design. And consider (this may be the ultimate question): how can we intelligently propose that this is a random universe when life itself is beyond the scope of a materialistic science to examine and design is the only reasonable answer to what we know and experience about our universe?

There is overwhelming evidence of a super-mind (God) who designed it. That is unless, as I have said, you have an already predetermined agenda that denies the possibility of a designer and excludes him from your unreasonable mental games.

Would you believe that a vehicle's combustion engine showed convincing evidence that it was designed or would you insist it had evolved by chance? No, come on, we all believe it had a designer. You wouldn't even believe that the engine showed up one day after billions of years of hit and miss random tries by an unintelligent substance, would you? Likewise, and a billion times more likely, is that this astonishing brain of ours was designed.

Let Me Offer Two Analogies:

1. If a tornado ripped through a junk metal yard, rearranging the trash and metals as it went, what are the chances that it would have created a fully functioning fighter jet as it exited the yard? You are, I believe, smart enough to believe that would never happen. And if it did, it would be a kindergarten achievement compared to the complex design that we see in our planet, ourselves, and the universe. And if you gave the tornado an infinite amount of time to keep churning and produce the fighter jet, it would still be an impossibility. Chance does not create design, purpose and intelligence.

2. If a monkey typed forever on a typewriter, what are the chances that it would finally type the works of Shakespeare — punctuation and all? Nada! None! Isn't it more likely that the monkey would produce an eternity of gibberish? If the universe and all that is in it were left to chance happenings, we would have a nonfunctioning universe or none at all. (Unbelievably this monkey at a typewriter analogy is used as an analogy to convince us that randomness, given enough time, would produce the intricate design we find in the universe. Really?).

Three significant points:

- Random acts never produce designed results of any significance. The idea in randomness is that it is the opposite of design and order, not its super-creator.

- Nor do chance happenings ever produce life and a universe that supports life. We have, instead, strong evidence of an intelligent mind. (I would even say inescapable evidence of an intelligent mind!)

- Again, an infinite amount of time does not change the outcome or nature of random chance happenings. The monkey would never do it.

Of course, you should find it incredible that a human brain arrived one day, complete and fully functional, operating all the above systems without a smidgin of intelligence being involved. A principle called *intelligent life* explains it, of course.

The Rest of Creation

Some of the trees I see every day as I hike in the Hill Country are oaks, and contained in their acorns are all a developing tree needs to guide it into becoming an oak tree. And it's not a cloning system, either. Every oak is different to some degree, but all are oaks. There are different designs in trees as well. How many trees our world contains, though unknown to me, is staggering. That acorn is nature's little reminder to me of design everywhere.

My hearing funnels to me even more evidence. The birds I hear singing in the morning — from the black tufted titmouse, to the cardinal and the mocking bird — open up yet another intricate process of design and purpose for me to witness. The evidence is overwhelmingly convincing.

1973 — A Revolutionary Discovery

"The Anthropic Principle[11]"

All of the above reasoning and evidence may have been sufficient to convince you that the universe has an intelligent designer. You may, by now, be looking at the words of Genesis 1:1, "In the beginning God created the heavens and the earth," with a burgeoning faith. But if not, here is a discovery from physics and cosmology that should flag you that there has been a revolution in science that amounts also to an embarrassment and a death blow to the philosophy of materialism (the belief that everything in our universe is some form of randomly formed matter — forget intelligence).

As a result of the discovery we are about to examine, the burden of proof is now solidly in the hands of atheistically motivated philosophers and scientists to show that our universe did not have a designer. It no longer rests in the hands of theologians, as it once did, to prove the universe had a designer. A secular, materialistic philosophy has for centuries sought to persuade us that Genesis 1:1 was simply a myth and not the truth. Friedrich Nietzsche summed it up for materialistic science with his drama-filled pronouncement in 1885, "God is Dead." Nietzsche had a mental breakdown in 1889 at the age of 45 and died at the age of 56 in 1900. Nietzsche is dead. News Break: God is still alive and doing fine!

---

[11] The word "anthropic" comes from the Greek word for man, *anthropos*. It was Carter's principle that the universe was created for man and shows evidence of a distinct purpose and, of course, intricate design. Carter coined the phrase "anthropic principle" and then, in his lecture, showed convincing evidence for this conclusion. The precise values of the four forces alone made this conclusion a matter of fact, not unsubstantiated theory.

Shock Waves

In 1973, Brandon Carter of Cambridge University, who is widely regarded as a cosmologist and astrophysicist, delivered a shock to the scientific community. It was at the conference that was convened to celebrate the 500th birthday of Copernicus. (Copernicus was the first to discover that the sun, not the earth, was the center of our universe).

Concerns had been brewing in some scientists' minds prior to Carter's lecture, which finally gave all these concerns full disclosure. For 500 years, Copernicus's discovery had been widely interpreted by atheistic and agnostic minds (and by many others, too, including some theologians) as clear evidence that the Genesis account of creation was, as a result of Copernicus's discovery, at least under suspicion because man no longer seemed to be the reason for the creation of the universe. The universe clearly revolved around the sun, not around man, who Bertrand Russell (the scientist/atheist) had maintained was nothing but a "curious accident in a backwater."

However, not so fast — as we shall see from the following findings.

In a very technical, yet convincing manner, Carter related the evidence for what he called *the anthropic principle*. There were several irrefutable facts that Carter laid bare.

Here, for our purposes, are the takeaway points.

Takeaways

1. Life would not be seen in our universe today without the five basic forces needed for human life to exist and thrive and having been in place from the moment of life's first appearance.

2. Carter also showed that from the very first nanosecond of the creation (the latest name for that moment is the "Big Bang"), not just the appearance of life in the universe, but the exact values

for the strengths of the universe's five basic forces (the electromagnetic, the weak and the strong nuclear forces, the Higgs field, and gravity[12] — also called constants because they must be constantly in effect) had to be in place for us to have the universe we have now.

3. He showed that anything other than these exact values for each of the forces (which we can accurately measure today) would have produced a vastly different universe and one in which life, for example, could not exist. Physicists could never explain why these forces existed in these precise values. This reasoning makes sense because what we have now in our universe must determine what would be needed at the beginning to produce today's universe.

4. This also had the effect of turning the *interpretation* (not the truth) of Copernicus's discovery upside down. It was commonly concluded that Copernicus had dealt the death blow to the biblical belief that man was the center and prime reason for the universe. Conclusions to new ideas often are accepted too fast. Carter's lecture reinstated the rationale for believing that humans could very well be the reason and purpose for the creation of the universe because the precise values (ratios) of the forces would have to be what they are to make life possible. On this count, Genesis chapters 1-3, which indicate man is the

---

[12] These five forces (well known to physicists and cosmologists), which are constantly operating in our universe and without which it would not exist, perform the following tasks: 1. electromagnetism is responsible for all electrical and magnetic functions and for chemistry and light; 2. the strong nuclear force holds protons and neutrons together in the center or nucleus of an atom; 3. the weak nuclear force is needed for some forms of radioactivity; 4. the Higgs field creates the mass in subatomic particles; and 5. gravity keeps us from floating off into space and guides all the planets as they whirl through space. Each of these appear in our universe in extremely precise values, ratios or percentages and the slightest tinkering with their values would wreak havoc and we would not have life or a universe that would support it.

purpose for the creation, would now no longer be under suspicion. Ouch! That reversed the thinking of centuries.

5. **In plainer words, what Carter demonstrated in his highly technical analysis was: the universe was expressly created for life and with mankind in mind, just like the Genesis account indicated — and this from the very beginning.** That life and mankind could have been a chance happening is, in itself, now way beyond credibility. We have dealt with chance happenings already! This was like the nail that sealed the coffin.

6. His argument and accurate technical deductions have not been shown to be inaccurate to this day.

7. These findings sent tremors through all current philosophic and scientific ideas of a random universe, mainly because they were "scientific." A universe that developed by random selection (chance happenings), including the remarkable "accident" of the human (as the prominent atheist Bertrand Russel called man's appearance in the universe) was, after all, clearly no accident at all.

8. The most reasonable conclusion from Carter's studies is that an intelligence had a design and purpose planned for the universe from the very beginning. Who that intelligence is cannot be determined from the evidence he presented.

9. It is no longer intellectually or scientifically unreasonable to believe in the biblical record. Because of the evidence we have amassed, faith in it has been raised to the status of the most intelligent belief about our origins.

10. The burden of proof that this universe is a random, chance happening now lies solidly at the feet of atheistic and agnostic scientists and these folk have their work cut out for them.

What an astounding reversal and embarrassment this discovery and its implications of a universe finely tuned for man's existence has been to the widely accepted philosophies that have underpinned some scientists' beliefs. Since the days when the influence of two publications resulted in dominating scientific and philosophical thought — namely, Descartes' *Meditations on First Philosophy* in 1641 and Newton's *Opticks* in 1704 — the evidence has been mounting in favor of a designed universe and not a random one. Now the evidence has become conclusive.

Can I ask you to decide for yourself whether the evidence in our universe points to an intelligent source or not? As you might surmise, the evidence from design has gone a long way to rocking the foundation of Darwinian *evolution* and its principles of natural selection, as we will see more fully in a future discussion.

Surely, you may rightly state, we should have heard of this by now, some 47 years later, and surely it would be taught in our colleges and universities. Again, not so fast.

Science Responds

And what has been the response of science to the revelations of Carter at the conference in 1973? Science does not easily give up and, in effect, has said we are not finished with this yet. No need to rewrite the text books. Rather, let's keep updating the world with our progress. Reasonable? Only if these scientists are really onto something. They believe or hope they are. We will see! Read on.

They are focusing their attention on two paths of investigation before they fail and would have to concede (which I'm convinced they will never do). Don't hold your breath as it will take as long as they feel impelled to keep trying, which may be a very long time. In the meantime, further evidence of the veracity of Carter's "Anthropic Principle" is piling up and further consolidates its conclusions. These scientists are also hard at work.

This whole turn of events has embarrassed science, too. The scientific theories and systems, which had no room for God and were thought to prove for all intelligent humans that they had presided over his death and that all intelligent people had got the message of his demise, were now on life support. Science, they were sure, could explain the origin and evolution of the universe without God.

These believers don't want to talk about the *Anthropic Principle* or its revolutionary effects. They are hopeful to again silence the need for God in all explanations of the universe. They want the two thoughts of a God and his creating the heavens and earth to once again be regarded by intelligent people as an ancient myth and nothing more. That's one reason why the *Anthropic Principle* is not being hailed as an amazing revolution in philosophic and scientific thought and taught for its true worth in higher education. "Don't rewrite the text books. Just give us more time to topple the *Anthropic Principle*" seems to be the plan.

A Theory of Everything

The first path of action to try and topple the *Anthropic Principle* is to call for a "time out" for more work to be done on discovering how to unify all five constant forces into one. If that could be done, it would reduce the odds of chance being able to land on one force with the right value or strength, rather than five forces each with their right values or strengths — the mathematical chances of which is astronomical. Chance could then become a more acceptable possibility for those who still insist on believing there is no God and no intelligence and purposeful planning behind the creation of the universe. One force rather than five is, therefore, the goal — what scientists like Dr. Don Lincoln are calling "The Theory of Everything"[13].

    A. If and when (two questions that seem very unlikely) they achieve this unification of the five forces (electromagnetic, the weak and strong nuclear forces, the Higgs field and gravity) or at least the results of their work look like a genuine possibility, they will, no doubt, call out, "Bingo!" Why? Because they will have hopefully reduced the mathematical challenge that mere chance would have had to face in that moment of the universe's beginning.

    B. But even if a unifying of the five forces could be accomplished (and that is highly unlikely), it would not explain how this one unified force came to be there in the first place. Problem of refuting the evidence from design — still unsolved!

    C. Please note: It would, of course, open up yet more debates on how, what or "who" designed the five forces or the one unified force and for what purpose and how did intelligence

---

[13] A thorough explanation of this theory and a rundown on its progress is in *The Theory of Everything, The Quest to Explain All Reality*, published as a transcript to Professor Don Lincoln's course in the Great Courses series, <u>wwwthegteartcourses.com</u>.

enter the picture, which has never been satisfactorily explained and remains in the field of unknowns.

D. We would still be asking whether the universe came into being by design. (Heaven forbid, since that would open up the flood gates to the reasonable admission that there was a designer!) Or whether it came about by a random accident (the only other option for atheists who must get rid of a designer). It would only shift the problem (design or no design) one step further back and leave it as still the core issue to be reckoned with. We would have then made progress back to where we started. Nor, does it explain why and how such a unity would nullify Carter's *Anthropic Principle* that is clear evidence of purposeful design.

E. However, this call for a time out would be a "God-send" (sorry!) while these scientists work on their speculations, the reality of which lies only in the imagination of their scientific minds. This, as you can see, enables them to hold up the sign saying, "We are not done yet. Wait!" But science will never be done since first, it is always a work in progress and second, they have still to know far more than they already know about a universe far too complex for the human mind to fully grasp. We can only gaze with wonder and awe at its complex magnificence and its overwhelming design.

F. Progress toward a solid answer? Anyone can call for a time out, but is it a logically legal move for those who have no facts to support their speculations? Would it not be more honest for them to admit the *Anthropic Principle* is indeed an embarrassment to their theories of a randomly created universe? As I said, we are back to where we started: overwhelming evidence of design.

Many Universes

The second path is to fall back on yet another more unbelievable speculation — at least in my thinking. You be the judge. In the mean time, we must, however, give credit to those who invent these amazing speculations. Here we are then, again calling for the necessity of yet another time-out on fact-less grounds.

    A. What is this request for a time out all about? In order for them to arrive at the precise values needed for the five constants to give us our universe by random selection. Mathematically speaking, there would need to be billions of attempts at randomly formed universes, one of which might luck upon the right combination of the five basic forces. All kinds of suggestions are being made of how these multiple universes would likely be formed — parallel universes, baby universes, bubble universes; and no doubt, there will be many other suggestions — all pure imagination, fact-less.

    B. Think of it: even a slight percentage off for any one of the five constants and disaster would strike — life would be impossible and that attempt at a life sustaining universe would bite the dust.

    C. As has been pointed out in *Universes* by John Leslie, 1989, in order to settle on the exact values of the five constants, we could have attempts that ended in: a universe composed of helium, or a universe with no protons or atoms, or one without stars, or one that failed to develop beyond the first few moments of its existence. Or, if the hydrogen atom did not contain its unique property that makes water lighter in its frozen form (lighter than its liquid form), it would mean our oceans would all freeze from the bottom up and our world would be nothing but ice. Conditions other than the five basic forces being in the form we find them in our universe could cause havoc.

D. In fact, as Glynn reminds us (see Patrick Glynn, *God, the Evidence* 1999, pages 29ff, if you want more detail), Frederick Hoyle (astronomer, mathematician, and astrophysicist) has summed it all up well with this thought: the universe had to know in advance what it was to be before it even began to be. The evidence for intelligent purposeful design is inescapable.

E. If we don't believe in a creator God, what we are being asked to believe seems to be something like these words that I have put into the mouths of those, now desperate, scientists: "In order to try and convince you that you should put your faith in our work as scientists who feel it necessary to reject the idea of a creator God, we still have to admit we actually have no real solid facts to back up our speculations. So we are asking you to consider our speculations as the most likely explanation of how the universe came into being." Is that more reasonable and intelligent than believing in the face of such overwhelming evidence of intelligent, purposeful design — that intelligence in the form of a deity created the heavens and the earth?

F. The speculation that billions of other universes — all hoping to be what we have today by random happenstance — are the solution to defeating the implications of the *Anthropic Principle* was first inspired by Edwin Hubble. He observed in 1927 what came to be called the "red shift mystery" — light shifting in the direction of the red end of the spectrum, suggesting the universe was constantly expanding, which could be the observation of other universes racing away from ours. This lead to the assumption that there may be many of these escaping universes seen by the color change feature.

G. Then in 1964, two Bell Laboratories scientists observed that cosmic radiation came from all directions in space. They were working on satellite communication systems and it was soon concluded by cosmologists that this cosmic radiation (which was to the scientists an annoying sound) was really an echo from the Big Bang billions of years earlier when the universe was formed. This is now considered to be as near as we have come to proof of the Big Bang theory. Putting these two observations together quickly led to the theory of the Big Bang being the beginning of our universe and the escaping universes the answer to how billions of universes randomly hit on the right combinations for one universe to create and nurture life as we have it today.

H. Admittedly these conclusions from the observations are full of assumptions. Assumptions are not proof of anything; they are working theories at best. Therefore, the "time out" could be either valid or invalid. However, please note: scientists have made many good assumptions and deserve our respect for these, so I am not trying to take anything away from them. But I am also not forgetting that science is a work in progress. What else might be found? We cannot forget that science proceeds "one funeral after another" when we are trying to decide where to put our faith. Fair? Is this heading for another funeral? Factually, we don't know; but we do not have anything to falsify the solid facts of the *Anthropic Principle*.

It's time to ask, "What if they do find other universes? Has it, without doubt, proved their theory that chance can and has produced this amazingly designed universe?" Not by a long shot! The real argument that we still have to address, no matter what is discovered, is whether random, happy accidents — even trillions of them — hit on the countless trillions of precise choices that would have to be made for life (something the complexity of which is not as yet understood) to come into existence and for it all to result in the creation of everything in our universe as we know it today? There are literally countless chances for mistakes on this hypothetical road. We are back to the real issue. The overwhelming evidence of intelligent, purposeful design in the universe cannot be dismissed! It is a fact. So "time outs" to find another candidate that just might be a possibility, while still not facing the facts we now clearly see, is refusing to acknowledge the intelligence, purpose and design that is overwhelmingly telling us how our universe must be understood.

Think once more of the monkey at the typewriter. It bangs away at the keys — let's say one stroke per second. In ten minutes, it faces at least 15,000 chances of making a mistake. And every time it happened to hit the right key, the next wrong choice would cancel the success and it would have to start again! If it were you blind folded, not the monkey, would you like to play that game with these odds demanding you had to hit the right keys trillions of times in succession or each wrong stroke would send you back to start all over again? If random strokes could create this universe, chance would be God, and the Bible would need to be rewritten with praise for the God of Chance. We would then be back to worshipping an idol, called unintelligence.

Astoundingly there is no proof — only speculations built on possibilities — for all these imaginary universes. They exist only in the fertile imaginations of these clever scientists. Does this fall into the category called "science fiction"?

In Conclusion

Let's Focus On Intelligence

Where did intelligence come from? There are only two answers: either from an intelligent source or an unintelligent source. It is profoundly illogical and begs belief to say that unintelligence can create intelligence — certainly not on the overwhelming scale of intelligent design seen in this universe.

Just think of the astounding inventions and exploits we humans have made. We have lived in space and built intricate systems that were unimaginable. Then ask, "Did all the billions of brain connections needed for such intelligent discoveries and inventions (*all* of them, not some, and each in the right order) happen by natural selection and its parent, chance? As I have said, the irreducible complexity needed for our cells to function and intelligence to happen is something even Darwin said would negate his theory of evolution.

The "design" argument we are using was historically seen to be finally dismissed after Darwin's publication of *The Origin of the Species* in 1859. It has come back with force to be the undeniable contender for an explanation of the origin of the universe. Why? Because we now see — almost daily — more compelling and overwhelming evidence in micro and macro studies of our universe. We also know the universe will not function without its intricate design. Nor can we live without being dependent on the design we find in our human systems and in our universe. We would die if it failed.

Because of the scientific equipment we now have, we are able to see more of the intelligent design in and around us, and more evidence of this intricate mind-boggling design is on its way.

But let's not forget, we still don't fully understand life. Life is the gift from the ultimate Designer to his creation and is the only logical answer for its appearance. Therefore, for those who still want to deny or sideline the overwhelming evidence for intelligent, purposeful design in our universe, the question that ominously looms over them is, "Where did life itself come from?" The question of life is the biggest elephant remaining in their room. Intelligence, not unintelligence, is the only choice for all questions of origin that will make any sense of our universe.

Of course, the argument from design was never really silenced or proved to be invalid. It was denied with inadequate arguments, not evidence. Now, in the face of the evidence, we have only one sensible answer: the heavens and the earth give undeniable evidence of intelligence, purpose and design. Conclusion: there must be a designer! Now we can say with confidence, the great apologist and theologian William Paley was right!

Let's Focus on the Implausible Nature of Random Happenings

At the obvious risk of redundancy, let me repeat. Randomness in any form would amount to believing that trillions upon trillions upon trillions of chance happenings all...

- fell into place
- at the right time
- in the right order
- with the right values
- supported by the right constants necessary for life itself to be possible
- and also for life to have the qualities to make it function successfully and consistently
- in a vast macro and micro universe
- without any intelligence or predesigned purpose

... to believe that this is the most plausible explanation of the origin of our universe. Who do these people think we are? Gullible idiots?

Random selection, used to explain our universe, is science fiction.

Let's Focus on What Chance Cannot Do

What is more, it wouldn't take billions of years for all this design in the universe to happen by chance. **It would never happen!** Chance cannot create order and design, period. Especially created and maintained on such an astronomical scale.

So, if someone asks you to believe this obvious impossibility and they happen to be the world's greatest scientific mind and have dozens of doctoral degrees to boot, you would be very foolish to believe them.

Let's Focus on Whether We Can Happily Live Knowing We Are Creatures of Chance?

If life is a chance happening, what does that mean for us?

It means we are not designed with a purpose and life has no purpose beyond what we devise for our own lives. When we find no purpose for our lives (because of this belief), the logical choice is to exit and save ourselves the troubles we face. Put another way, life itself becomes meaningless.

Acceptance of depression, despair and suicide would then become meaningful. This was the supposed "wisdom" of the French philosophers behind the concept of the *Theatre of the Absurd*. It was an absurd conclusion of how to live meaninglessly that was logically deduced from an absurd philosophy but consistent with the belief that there is no God and that we are just accidents in a process of evolution. Thank God — yes God! — that this is not true and not our only alternative because we can now see clearly that there is a designer behind his creation and life finds its purpose in a relationship of trust in him. People can't live with the thought they are only animate things. Being designed means we have a purpose. Without a purpose in life, we all begin to fall apart and plunge into despair, as I have seen too many times. The solution is to find and engage in your created purpose and establish your unique purpose. A healthy life and self-image are then restored. Fortunately for us, we are designed for a purpose. Design implies a purpose and that purpose was the reason for the creation in the first place.

Scientists have proved to us that if they ingeniously use and follow the dependable laws and design we find in our universe, they can create wonders and things beyond our imagination. This can make us think of science as the greatest human advance in all history… but mark this, only because it discovers yet more and more of the mind-boggling design in our universe and uses that knowledge to our astonishment and benefit. Purpose, design and intelligence is a scientist's tool kit. Lesson? If scientists (or anyone) think they are products of an unintelligent accident, then in order to live successfully, act as though you believe the opposite.

We therefore ask, can these ingenious minds expect us to believe that unintelligence and a lack of design is the answer to our origins when intelligence and design is what leads them to such amazing discoveries? There is an obvious unexplained inconsistency here. We can't live happily with such big inconsistencies or with the knowledge that unintelligent forces are where we came from.

Will unintelligence and random happenings lead us to living a better life? Who believes that? Of course it won't. What's most glaring is the conclusion that none of us can live our own lives without using intelligence, planning, design and forethought. They are a part of who we are. Every time scientists create some new marvel, we should be thankful that it shows us again how wonderfully designed is the universe they have to work with, and likewise their own mental ingenuity that they use. They can't live without using what their theories of unintelligent origins cannot explain and they cannot deny them.

If any one of us really did believe we were an unplanned, undesigned accident, we should be among the most nervous people alive. All of our achievements and our very existence would be subject to the winds of thoughtless chance, and a random move on its part could destroy us all with all our achievements anytime, any day. To believe in a chance origin is to face a future full of fear and uncertainty. That alone can incapacitate any person. To believe we are here by design and in the hands of a loving God makes life worth living and it can be lived peacefully and confidently. Faith in God beats a faith in no God any day.

Take designed functioning out of the thousands of daily happenings involving the use of our bodies and we will not live long enough to know it. If the universe were not designed purposefully and dependably and built on the constancy of laws from the very first nanosecond (as the *Anthropic Principle* has shown), life itself would be impossible. Here's the only upside to randomness: The struggling math student would be able to return an answer that 2 plus 2 equals 29 — and pass.

Don't we get up every morning and depend on our human bodies to function dependably — all according to their design? Are we not amazingly designed? I think we all act as though we are, even if some try to convince themselves and others that we are not. So, if you still believe in a random universe, live as though you don't.

Next Question:
Of great importance is sorting out what we believe about ourselves. I'll discuss this in my next book.

Bibliography

For those who wish further information, this short list will help expand what is in this book and provide a copious list of resources.

Behe, Michael J., *Darwins Black Box - The Biochemical Challenge to Evolution* (Free Press, A Division of Simon & Schuster, Inc., 2006) Details of our biochemical make up in support of intelligent design.

Brown, Colin, *Philosophy and the Christian Faith, A Historical Sketch from the Middle Ages to the Present Day* (Intervarsity Press, 1968) A survey of philosophical thought leading up to the works of Francis Schaefer.

Carey, George, *Why I Believe in a Personal God, The Credibility of Faith in a Doubting Culture* (Harold Shaw Publisher, 1989) An Archbishop of Canterbury discusses his faith.

Collins, Francis S., *The Language of God, A Scientist Presents Evidence for Belief* (Free Press, A Division of Simon and Schuster, 2006) Collins was head of the Genome Project and discusses Faith and Science in a compelling way.

Glynn, Patrick, *God the Evidence - The Reconciliation of Faith and Reason in a Post-secular World* (Three Rivers Press, 1999) The reasons why Patrick found faith in God. Discusses a not-so-random universe.

Guillen, Michael, *Can a Smart Person Believe in* God (Nelson Books, 2004) A theoretical Physicist discusses the synthesis of reason and faith.

Hawking, Stephen, *A Brief History of Time - From the Big Bang to Black Holes* (Bantam Books, 1990) A famous theoretical Physicist presents an opposing view to Michael Guillen; secular instead of faith-bound.

Lincoln, Don, *The Theory of Everything, The Quest to Explain All Reality* (The Great Courses, 2017) A Great Courses Transcript presents the latest search for a way to deny the sense of Genesis, Chapter One, and the mounting evidence of intelligent design.

Morris, Thomas V., editor, *God and the Philosophers* (Oxford University Press, 1994) Philosophers who found faith instead of losing it.

Nicholi, Jr, Armand M., *The Question of God - C. S. Lewis and Sigmond Freud Debate God, Love, Sex and the Meaning of Life* (Free Press, a Division of Simon & Schuster, 2002) A debate between C. S. Lewis and Sigmund Freud that begins with the subject of God.

Paley, William M., *Natural Theology* or *Evidences of the Existence and Attributes of the Deity Collected from the Appearances of Nature* (Suzeteo Enterprises) An old classic whose thesis is on the front line of debate, today. This book is in the public domain; it was originally written in 1809 and this edition reflects the work as published in 1860. The foreword and cover are copyrighted in 2012.

Pearcey, Nancy, *Total Truth, Liberating Christianity from Its Cultural Captivity* (Crossway, 2004, 2005) An apologetic approach to the question of God and other relevant issues.

Schaeffer, Francis, *The Complete Works of Francis Schaeffer, A Christian Worldview, Volume 1, A Christian View of Philosophy and Culture* (Crossway, 1987) This covers a vast range of subjects, but book one, *The God Who Is There*, is a classic read.

Sire, James M., *The Universe Next Door* (Intervarsity Press, 1988) A world view catalogue. An excellent introduction to major world views for a wide understanding of how we have arrived at the secular influences of today.

www.ingramcontent.com/pod-product-compliance
Lightning Source LLC
Chambersburg PA
CBHW061301040426
42444CB00010B/2452